20 best chocolate cookie recipes

Houghton Mifflin Harcourt
Boston • New York • 2013

Copyright © 2013 by General Mills, Minneapolis, Minnesota. All rights reserved.

For information about permission to reproduce selections from this book, write to Permissions, Houghton Mifflin Harcourt Publishing Company, 215 Park Avenue South, New York, New York 10003.

www.hmhco.com

Cover photo: Outrageous Double Chocolate–White Chocolate Chunk Cookies (page 10)

General Mills
Food Content and Relationship Marketing Director: Geoff Johnson
Food Content Marketing Manager: Susan Klobuchar
Senior Editor: Grace Wells
Kitchen Manager: Ann Stuart
Recipe Development and Testing: Betty Crocker Kitchens
Photography: General Mills Photography Studios and Image Library

Houghton Mifflin Harcourt
Publisher: Natalie Chapman
Editorial Director: Cindy Kitchel
Executive Editor: Anne Ficklen
Associate Editor: Heather Dabah
Managing Editor: Rebecca Springer
Production Editor: Kristi Hart
Cover Design: Chrissy Kurpeski
Book Design: Tai Blanche

ISBN 978-0-544-31472-6
Printed in the United States of America

The Betty Crocker Kitchens seal guarantees success in your kitchen. Every recipe has been tested in America's Most Trusted Kitchens™ to meet our high standards of reliability, easy preparation and great taste.

FIND MORE GREAT IDEAS AT
BettyCrocker.com

Dear Friends,

This new collection of colorful mini books has been put together with you in mind because we know that you love great recipes and enjoy cooking and baking but have a busy lifestyle. So every little book in the series contains just 20 recipes for you to treasure and enjoy. Plus, each book is a single subject designed in a bite-size format just for you—it's easy to use and is filled with favorite recipes from the Betty Crocker Kitchens!

All of the books are conveniently divided into short chapters so you can quickly find what you're looking for, and the beautiful photos throughout are sure to entice you into making the delicious recipes. In the series, you'll discover a fabulous array of recipes to spark your interest—from cookies, cupcakes and birthday cakes to party ideas for a variety of occasions. There's grilled foods, potluck favorites and even gluten-free recipes too.

You'll love the variety in these mini books—so pick one or choose them all for your cooking pleasure.

Enjoy and happy cooking!

Sincerely,

Betty Crocker

contents

Easy Drop Cookies
Quick-Mix Chocolate Cookies • 6
Chocolate Crinkles • 7
Double-Chocolate Oatmeal Cookies • 8
Best-Ever Chocolate Cookies • 9
Outrageous Double Chocolate–White
 Chocolate Chunk Cookies • 10

Frosted & Topped Cookies
Chocolate Sundae Cone Cookies • 12
Triple–Chocolate Chunk Cookies • 13
Chocolate Drop Cookies • 14
Fudgy Frosted Brownie Cookies • 15
Peanut Butter–Stuffed Chocolate Cookies • 16
Chocolate-Marshmallow Cookie Treats • 17
Oh-So-Good Chocolate Cherry Cookies • 18
Coconut-Chocolate-Almond Cookies • 19

Shaped Cookies
Mexican Hot Chocolate Cookies • 20
Chocolate-Toffee Crinkle Cookies • 21
Chocolate-Mint Layered Cookie Slices • 22
Chocolate-Peppermint Shortbread • 23
Simple Turtle Cookie Cups • 24
Whoopie Pies • 25
Chocolate-Mallow Cookie Pies • 26

Metric Conversion Guide • 28
Recipe Testing and Calculating Nutrition
 Information • 29

Easy Drop Cookies

Quick-Mix Chocolate Cookies

Prep Time: 20 Minutes • **Start to Finish:** 1 Hour 50 Minutes • Makes 2½ dozen cookies

- 1 box Betty Crocker SuperMoist® devil's food cake mix
- ⅓ cup vegetable oil
- 1 teaspoon vanilla
- 2 eggs
- ¼ cup sugar

1 Heat oven to 350°F. In large bowl, mix cake mix, oil, vanilla and eggs with spoon until dough forms.

2 Refrigerate dough 15 to 30 minutes or as needed for easier handling. Shape dough into 1-inch balls; roll in sugar. On ungreased cookie sheets, place balls about 2 inches apart.

3 Bake 9 to 11 minutes or until set. Cool 1 minute; remove from cookie sheets to cooling racks. Cool completely, about 30 minutes. Store tightly covered.

1 Cookie: Calories 90; Total Fat 3.5g (Saturated Fat 1g, Trans Fat 0g); Cholesterol 15mg; Sodium 125mg; Total Carbohydrate 13g (Dietary Fiber 0g); Protein 1g **Exchanges:** ½ Starch, ½ Other Carbohydrate, ½ Fat **Carbohydrate Choices:** 1

Chocolate Chip-Chocolate Cookies: Stir ⅔ cup miniature semisweet chocolate chips into the dough.

Chocolate Crinkles

Prep Time: 1 Hour • **Start to Finish:** 4 Hours • Makes 6 dozen cookies

2 cups granulated sugar
½ cup vegetable oil
2 teaspoons vanilla
4 oz unsweetened baking chocolate, melted, cooled
4 eggs
2 cups Gold Medal® all-purpose flour
2 teaspoons baking powder
½ teaspoon salt
1 cup powdered sugar

1 In large bowl, stir granulated sugar, oil, vanilla and chocolate until well mixed. Stir in eggs, one at a time. Stir in flour, baking powder and salt. Cover and refrigerate at least 3 hours.

2 Heat oven to 350°F. Grease cookie sheets with shortening or cooking spray, or line with cooking parchment paper.

3 In small bowl, place powdered sugar. Drop dough by teaspoonfuls into powdered sugar; roll around to coat. Shape into balls. On cookie sheets, place balls about 2 inches apart.

4 Bake 10 to 12 minutes or until almost no indentation remains when touched in center. Immediately remove from cookie sheets to cooling racks.

1 Cookie: Calories 70; Total Fat 2.5g (Saturated Fat 1g, Trans Fat 0g); Cholesterol 10mg; Sodium 35mg; Total Carbohydrate 10g (Dietary Fiber 0g); Protein 1g **Exchanges:** ½ Starch, ½ Fat **Carbohydrate Choices:** ½

Double-Chocolate Oatmeal Cookies

Prep Time: 20 Minutes • **Start to Finish:** 1 Hour 30 Minutes • Makes 3 dozen cookies

- 1 cup packed brown sugar
- ½ cup butter or margarine, softened
- ¾ cup Yoplait®* 99% Fat Free plain yogurt (from 2-lb container)
- 1 egg or ¼ cup fat-free egg product
- 1 teaspoon vanilla
- ⅓ cup unsweetened baking cocoa
- ⅔ cup Gold Medal all-purpose flour
- ⅔ cup Gold Medal whole wheat flour
- ½ teaspoon baking soda
- ¼ teaspoon salt
- 3 cups old-fashioned or quick-cooking oats
- ⅓ cup miniature semisweet chocolate chips or white chocolate chips

1 Heat oven to 350°F. In large bowl, mix sugar, butter, yogurt, egg and vanilla. Stir in remaining ingredients. Onto ungreased cookie sheet, drop dough by rounded tablespoonfuls about 2 inches apart.

2 Bake 11 to 13 minutes or until almost no indentation remains when touched. Immediately remove from cookie sheets to cooling racks.

1 Cookie: Calories 110 (Calories from Fat 35); Total Fat 4g (Saturated Fat 2g, Trans Fat 0g); Cholesterol 15mg; Sodium 60mg; Total Carbohydrate 17g (Dietary Fiber 2g); Protein 2g **Exchanges:** ½ Starch, ½ Other Carbohydrate, 1 Fat **Carbohydrate Choices:** 1

Tip Quick-cooking and old-fashioned rolled oats work equally well in this recipe. Quick-cooking oats are simply old-fashioned oats that have been ground to a finer texture. Use the old-fashioned oats if you prefer chewier cookies.

*Yoplait is a registered trademark of YOPLAIT MARQUES (France) used under license.

Best-Ever Chocolate Cookies

Prep Time: 50 Minutes • **Start to Finish:** 50 Minutes • Makes 3½ dozen cookies

- 1 cup butter or margarine, softened
- ¾ cup packed brown sugar
- ½ cup granulated sugar
- 2 eggs
- 1 cup Gold Medal all-purpose flour
- ½ cup unsweetened baking cocoa
- 1 teaspoon baking soda
- ¼ teaspoon salt
- 1 cup Fiber One® original bran cereal
- 1½ cups quick-cooking or old-fashioned oats
- ¾ cup white vanilla baking chips

1 Heat oven to 350°F. In large bowl, mix butter, sugars and eggs. In small bowl, mix flour, cocoa, baking soda and salt; stir into butter mixture. Stir in cereal, oats and baking chips.

2 Onto ungreased cookie sheets, drop dough by rounded tablespoonfuls about 2 inches apart.

3 Bake 9 minutes. Cool 1 to 2 minutes; remove from cookie sheets to cooling racks. Cool completely before storing in tightly covered container.

1 Cookie: Calories 120; Total Fat 6g (Saturated Fat 4g, Trans Fat 0g); Cholesterol 20mg; Sodium 95mg; Total Carbohydrate 15g (Dietary Fiber 1g); Protein 1g **Exchanges:** 1 Other Carbohydrate, 1 Fat **Carbohydrate Choices:** 1

Double Chocolate Cookies: Replace vanilla chips with semisweet or dark chocolate chips.

Outrageous Double Chocolate–White Chocolate Chunk Cookies

Prep Time: 1 Hour 25 Minutes • **Start to Finish:** 1 Hour 25 Minutes • Makes 2 dozen cookies

- 1 bag (24 oz) semisweet chocolate chips (4 cups)
- 1 package (6 oz) white chocolate baking bars
- 1 cup butter or margarine, room temperature
- 1 cup packed brown sugar
- 1 teaspoon vanilla
- 2 eggs
- 2½ cups Gold Medal all-purpose flour
- 1½ teaspoons baking soda
- ½ teaspoon salt
- 1 cup pecan or walnut halves

1 Heat the oven to 350°F. In 1-quart saucepan, heat 1½ cups of the chocolate chips over low heat, stirring constantly, until melted. Cool to room temperature, about 15 minutes, but do not allow chocolate to become firm. Meanwhile, cut white chocolate baking bars into ¼- to ½-inch chunks; set aside.

2 In large bowl, beat butter, brown sugar and vanilla with electric mixer on medium speed until light and fluffy. Beat in eggs and melted chocolate until light and fluffy. With wooden spoon, stir in flour, baking soda and salt. Stir in remaining 2½ cups chocolate chips, the white chocolate chunks and pecan halves.

3 For each cookie, spoon dough into ¼-cup dry-ingredient measuring cup and level off with knife. Onto ungreased cookie sheet, drop dough about 2 inches apart.

4 Bake 12 to 14 minutes or until set (centers will appear soft and moist). Cool 2 minutes; remove from cookie sheet to cooling rack.

1 Cookie: Calories 380; Total Fat 22g (Saturated Fat 12g, Trans Fat 0g); Cholesterol 40mg; Sodium 200mg; Total Carbohydrate 41g (Dietary Fiber 2g); Protein 4g **Exchanges:** 1 Starch, 1½ Other Carbohydrate, 4½ Fat **Carbohydrate Choices:** 3

Tip To save time, use 1 cup white vanilla baking chips (from a 12-ounce bag) instead of chopping the white chocolate baking bars.

Outrageous Double Chocolate Chunk Cookies: Use 1 package (5 oz) milk chocolate candy bar, cut into ¼- to ½-inch chunks, instead of the white chocolate baking bars.

Chopping White Chocolate Baking Bar Place the baking bar on a cutting board. Using a knife, chop the bar into ¼- to ½-inch chunks.

Measuring Cookie Dough Spoon dough into a ¼-cup dry-ingredient measuring cup and level off with a knife.

Frosted & Topped Cookies

Chocolate Sundae Cone Cookies

Prep Time: 1 Hour 20 Minutes • **Start to Finish:** 1 Hour 20 Minutes • Makes 2½ dozen cookies

- 1 bag (11.5 or 12 oz) semisweet chocolate chunks (2 cups), divided
- ½ cup butter or margarine, softened
- 1 egg
- 1 pouch (1 lb 1.5 oz) Betty Crocker chocolate chip cookie mix
- 1 cup white vanilla baking chips (6 oz)
- 4 sugar cones, coarsely crushed (about 1¼ cups)
- ½ cup dry-roasted peanuts, coarsely chopped

1 Heat oven to 350°F. In large microwavable bowl, microwave 1 cup chocolate chunks uncovered on High 1 minute to 1 minute 30 seconds, stirring every 30 seconds, until melted and smooth. Add butter; using spoon, beat until blended. Add egg; beat until combined. Add cookie mix; stir until soft dough forms. Stir in remaining 1 cup chocolate chunks and the vanilla baking chips. Gently stir in crushed cones just until combined.

2 Onto ungreased cookie sheets, drop dough by 2 tablespoonfuls per cookie; flatten tops slightly. Sprinkle with peanuts, pressing lightly into dough. Bake 8 to 10 minutes or until puffed and dry on tops (centers will be very soft). Cool 3 minutes; remove from cookie sheets to cooling racks. Cool completely before storing in tightly covered container.

1 Cookie: Calories 220; Total Fat 12g (Saturated Fat 7g, Trans Fat 0g); Cholesterol 15mg; Sodium 125mg; Total Carbohydrate 26g (Dietary Fiber 1g); Protein 2g **Exchanges:** 1 Starch, ½ Other Carbohydrate, 2½ Fat **Carbohydrate Choices:** 2

Tip Sugar cones add crunchy texture, so they should not be finely crushed. To keep them coarse, crush by hand into ½- to 1-inch pieces.

Triple-Chocolate Chunk Cookies

Prep Time: 35 Minutes • **Start to Finish:** 1 Hour 40 Minutes • Makes 3 dozen cookies

1 Heat oven to 375°F. In large bowl, beat brown sugar, butter and egg with electric mixer on medium speed, or mix with spoon. Stir in flour, baking soda and salt (dough will be soft). Stir in nuts, 4 oz bittersweet chocolate, 4 oz sweet chocolate and 4 oz white chocolate. Onto ungreased cookie sheet, drop dough by rounded tablespoonfuls about 2 inches apart.

2 Bake 8 to 10 minutes or until light golden brown. Cool 1 to 2 minutes; remove from cookie sheets to cooling racks. Cool completely, about 30 minutes.

3 In small saucepan, heat 1 teaspoon shortening and 3 oz bittersweet chocolate over low heat, stirring constantly, until chocolate is melted and smooth; remove from heat. Repeat with 1 teaspoon shortening and 3 oz sweet chocolate; repeat with 1 teaspoon shortening and 3 oz white chocolate to make 3 separate glazes.

4 Dip ½-inch edge of each cookie into each glaze, allowing each glaze to completely set before dipping into next glaze and rotating dipped edge of cookie for each type of glaze. Place cookies on waxed paper to allow glazes to set.

Cookies
- 1½ cups packed brown sugar
- 1 cup butter or margarine, softened
- 1 egg
- 2¼ cups Gold Medal all-purpose flour
- 1 teaspoon baking soda
- ½ teaspoon salt
- 1 cup chopped nuts
- 4 oz bittersweet baking chocolate, chopped
- 4 oz sweet baking chocolate, chopped
- 4 oz white chocolate baking bar, chopped

Three-Chocolate Glaze
- 3 teaspoons shortening
- 3 oz bittersweet baking chocolate
- 3 oz sweet baking chocolate
- 3 oz white chocolate baking bar

1 Cookie: Calories 225; Total Fat 13g (Saturated Fat 7g, Trans Fat 0); Cholesterol 20mg; Sodium 115mg; Total Carbohydrate 26g (Dietary Fiber 1g); Protein 2g **Exchanges:** 1 Starch, 1 Fruit, 2 Fat **Carbohydrate Choices:** 2

Tip Use a spring-handled ice-cream scoop to drop the dough. This ensures the cookies are the same size, which means they'll bake evenly.

Chocolate Drop Cookies

Prep Time: 1 Hour • **Start to Finish:** 1 Hour 30 Minutes • Makes 3 dozen cookies

Cookies

1 cup granulated sugar
½ cup butter or margarine, softened
⅓ cup buttermilk
1 teaspoon vanilla
1 egg
2 oz unsweetened baking chocolate, melted, cooled
1¾ cups Gold Medal all-purpose flour
½ teaspoon baking soda
½ teaspoon salt

Frosting

2 oz unsweetened baking chocolate
2 tablespoons butter or margarine
2 cups powdered sugar
3 tablespoons hot water

1 Heat oven to 400°F. Grease cookie sheets with shortening or spray with cooking spray. In large bowl, beat granulated sugar, ½ cup butter, the buttermilk, vanilla, egg and 2 oz chocolate with electric mixer on medium speed until smooth, or mix with spoon. Stir in flour, baking soda and salt.

2 Onto cookie sheets, drop dough by rounded tablespoonfuls about 2 inches apart.

3 Bake 8 to 10 minutes or until almost no indentation remains when touched in center. Immediately remove from cookie sheets to cooling racks. Cool completely, about 30 minutes.

4 In 2-quart saucepan, melt 2 oz chocolate and 2 tablespoons butter over low heat, stirring occasionally; remove from heat. Stir in powdered sugar and hot water until smooth. (If frosting is too thick, add more water, 1 teaspoon at a time. If frosting is too thin, add more powdered sugar, 1 tablespoon at a time.) Frost cooled cookies. Let stand until set.

1 Cookie: Calories 120 (Calories from Fat 45); Total Fat 5g (Saturated Fat 2.5g; Trans Fat 0); Cholesterol 15mg; Sodium 75mg; Total Carbohydrate 18g (Dietary Fiber 0g); Protein 1g **Exchanges:** ½ Starch, ½ Other Carbohydrate, 1 Fat **Carbohydrate Choices:** 1

Tip To quickly melt 2 ounces chocolate, place in a small microwavable container. Microwave on High 1 to 2 minutes, stirring every 30 seconds until melted and smooth.

Fudgy Frosted Brownie Cookies

Prep Time: 45 Minutes • **Start to Finish:** 1 Hour 15 Minutes • Makes 1½ dozen cookies

1 Heat oven to 350°F. Spray cookie sheets with cooking spray. In medium bowl, mix all cookie ingredients until well blended.

2 Onto cookie sheets, drop dough by rounded tablespoonfuls about 2 inches apart.

3 Bake 9 to 11 minutes or until set. Cool 2 minutes; remove from cookie sheets to cooling racks. Cool completely, about 30 minutes.

4 In 2-quart saucepan, melt chocolate and butter over low heat, stirring occasionally. Remove from heat. Stir in powdered sugar and 3 tablespoons of the hot water until smooth. (If frosting is too thick, add more water, 1 teaspoon at a time.) Spread frosting over cookies.

Cookies
- 1 cup Original Bisquick® mix
- ¾ cup granulated sugar
- ⅔ cup chopped pecans
- ½ cup unsweetened baking cocoa
- ½ cup sour cream
- 1 teaspoon vanilla
- 1 egg

Frosting
- 2 oz unsweetened baking chocolate
- 2 tablespoons butter or margarine
- 2 cups powdered sugar
- 3 to 4 tablespoons hot water

1 Cookie: Calories 200 (Calories from Fat 80); Total Fat 9g (Saturated Fat 3.5g, Trans Fat 0g); Cholesterol 20mg; Sodium 100mg; Total Carbohydrate 29g (Dietary Fiber 2g); Protein 2g **Exchanges:** ½ Starch, 1½ Other Carbohydrate, 1½ Fat **Carbohydrate Choices:** 2

Tip You can freeze frosted cookies tightly covered for up to 2 months.

Peanut Butter–Stuffed Chocolate Cookies

Prep Time: 1 Hour • **Start to Finish:** 1 Hour 30 Minutes • Makes 2½ dozen cookies

Cookies

- ½ cup butter or margarine, cut up
- 1 cup semisweet chocolate chips (6 oz)
- 2 tablespoons peanut butter
- 1 pouch (1 lb 1.5 oz) Betty Crocker chocolate chip cookie mix
- 1 egg
- 30 mini peanut butter crackers

Drizzle

- 1 cup peanut butter chips (6 oz)
- 1 to 2 teaspoons vegetable oil

1 In large microwavable bowl, microwave butter, chocolate chips and peanut butter uncovered on High 1 minute to 1 minute 30 seconds, stirring every 30 seconds, until melted and smooth. Stir in cookie mix and egg until well blended. Refrigerate dough 30 minutes or until firm enough to scoop.

2 Heat oven to 375°F. For each rounded measuring tablespoon dough, place 1 peanut butter cracker in center, forming dough into ball around cracker. On ungreased cookie sheets, place balls about 2 inches apart.

3 Bake 9 to 11 minutes or until tops are dry (cookies will still be soft). Cool 1 minute; remove from cookie sheets to cooling racks.

In 1-pint resealable food-storage plastic bag, place peanut butter chips and oil; seal bag. Microwave on High 1 minute, kneading bag after 30 seconds, until melted and smooth. Cut ⅛-inch slit diagonally across bottom corner of bag. Squeeze drizzle over cooled cookies. Let stand until set. Store in tightly covered container.

1 Cookie: Calories 180 (Calories from Fat 90); Total Fat 10g (Saturated Fat 4.5g, Trans Fat 0g); Cholesterol 15mg; Sodium 130mg; Total Carbohydrate 21g (Dietary Fiber 0g); Protein 2g **Exchanges:** ½ Starch, 1 Other Carbohydrate, 2 Fat **Carbohydrate Choices:** 1½

Tip If dough gets sticky while forming cookies, return to refrigerator for 10 to 15 minutes or until firm enough to handle.

Chocolate-Marshmallow Cookie Treats

Prep Time: 1 Hour • **Start to Finish:** 1 Hour • Makes 1½ dozen cookies

1 pouch (1 lb 1.5 oz) Betty Crocker double chocolate chunk cookie mix

Vegetable oil, water and egg called for on cookie mix pouch

18 large marshmallows

1 cup hot fudge topping

Betty Crocker candy sprinkles

1 Make cookie dough as directed on package. Bake at 350°F 10 to 12 minutes. Cut marshmallows in half using serrated knife. Immediately top each hot cookie with marshmallow, cut side down, pressing down firmly. Cool; remove from cookie sheets to cooling racks.

2 Microwave fudge topping on High 30 seconds or until warm. Spoon topping over each marshmallow-topped cookie. Top with candy sprinkles.

1 Cookie: Calories 240; Total Fat 8g (Saturated Fat 3.5g, Trans Fat 0g); Cholesterol 10mg; Sodium 190mg; Total Carbohydrate 40g (Dietary Fiber 0g); Protein 2g **Exchanges:** ½ Starch, 2 Other Carbohydrate, 1½ Fat **Carbohydrate Choices:** 2½

Tip Use cooking parchment paper to line cookie sheets and make cleanup a snap.

Oh-So-Good Chocolate Cherry Cookies

Prep Time: 1 Hour 10 Minutes • **Start to Finish:** 1 Hour 40 Minutes • Makes 3 dozen cookies

- 1 pouch (1 lb 1.5 oz) Betty Crocker double chocolate chunk cookie mix
- ¼ cup vegetable oil
- 2 tablespoons water
- 1 egg
- ¼ cup almonds, finely chopped
- 1 cup semisweet chocolate chips (from 12-oz. bag)
- ¼ cup whipping cream
- 36 maraschino cherries, from 2 jars, drained, pat dry

1 Heat oven to 350°F. In large bowl, stir cookie mix, oil, water and egg until soft dough forms. Stir in almonds. Onto ungreased cookie sheet, drop dough by rounded teaspoonfuls about 2 inches apart. Place 1 cherry on each cookie. Bake 8 to 10 minutes. Cool 1 minute; remove from cookie sheets to cooling racks.

2 Meanwhile, in small microwavable bowl, microwave chocolate chips and cream uncovered on High 30 to 45 seconds; stir until smooth. Spoon generous teaspoonful onto each cookie and spread over cookie. Allow chocolate to set until firm; about 30 minutes.

1 Cookie: Calories 110; Total Fat 5g (Saturated Fat 2g, Trans Fat 0g); Cholesterol 10mg; Sodium 65mg; Total Carbohydrate 16g (Dietary Fiber 0g); Protein 1g **Exchanges:** 1 Other Carbohydrate, 1 Fat **Carbohydrate Choices:** 1

Coconut-Chocolate-Almond Cookies

Prep Time: 30 Minutes • **Start to Finish:** 1 Hour • Makes 2 dozen cookies

1 pouch (1 lb 1.5 oz) Betty Crocker sugar cookie mix

⅓ cup unsweetened baking cocoa

½ cup butter, softened

1 egg

½ teaspoon almond extract

½ cup sliced almonds, toasted*

1 container (1 lb) Betty Crocker Rich & Creamy cream cheese frosting

1 teaspoon coconut extract

½ cup flaked coconut, toasted**

1 Heat oven to 375°F. In large bowl, stir cookie mix and cocoa until well blended. Add butter, egg and almond extract; stir until soft dough forms. Gently stir in almonds. Onto ungreased cookie sheet, drop dough by rounded tablespoonfuls about 2 inches apart.

2 Bake 12 minutes or until set. Remove from cookie sheet to cooling rack. Cool completely, about 30 minutes.

3 In medium bowl, stir frosting and coconut extract. Frost cookies. Sprinkle with coconut.

1 Cookie: Calories 229; Total Fat 10g (Saturated Fat 4g, Trans Fat 0); Cholesterol 0mg; Sodium 130mg; Total Carbohydrate 31g (Dietary Fiber 1g); Protein 2g **Exchanges:** ½ Starch, 1½ Other Carbohydrate, 2 Fat **Carbohydrate Choices:** 2

* To toast almonds, sprinkle in ungreased shallow pan. Bake uncovered at 350°F 6 to 10 minutes, stirring occasionally, until golden brown.

** To toast coconut, sprinkle in ungreased shallow pan. Bake at 350°F 4 to 6 minutes, stirring occasionally, until golden brown.

Shaped Cookies

Mexican Hot Chocolate Cookies

Prep Time: 1 Hour • **Start to Finish:** 1 Hour • Makes 4 dozen cookies

¼ cup sugar
¼ teaspoon ground cinnamon
½ cup butter or margarine
1 tablet Mexican hot chocolate drink mix (from 19-oz package)
1 pouch (1 lb 1.5 oz) Betty Crocker sugar cookie mix
1 egg
1 cup (6 oz) miniature semisweet chocolate chips

1 Heat oven to 375°F. In small bowl, mix sugar and cinnamon; set aside.

2 In 1-quart saucepan, melt butter and hot chocolate tablet over low heat, stirring constantly.

3 In large bowl, stir cookie mix, melted butter mixture and egg until soft dough forms. Stir in chocolate chips.

4 Shape dough into 1-inch balls; roll in cinnamon-sugar mixture. On ungreased cookie sheets, place balls about 2 inches apart.

5 Bake 10 to 12 minutes or until set (do not overbake). Cool 3 minutes; remove from cookie sheets to cooling racks. Store covered at room temperature.

1 Cookie: Calories 90; Total Fat 4.5g (Saturated Fat 2g, Trans Fat 0g); Cholesterol 10mg; Sodium 40mg; Total Carbohydrate 13g (Dietary Fiber 0g); Protein 0g **Exchanges:** 1 Other Carbohydrate, 1 Fat **Carbohydrate Choices:** 1

Chocolate-Toffee Crinkle Cookies

Prep Time: 1 Hour • **Start to Finish:** 1 Hour • Makes 2 dozen cookies

- 8 oz semisweet baking chocolate, chopped
- ¼ cup butter or margarine, cut up
- 1¼ cups Gold Medal all-purpose flour
- ¼ cup unsweetened baking cocoa
- ½ teaspoon baking soda
- ¼ teaspoon salt
- 1 cup sugar
- 2 eggs
- 1 teaspoon vanilla
- 1 bag (8 oz) toffee bits
- Sugar

1 In 1-quart saucepan, heat chocolate and butter over medium-low heat, stirring frequently, until chocolate is melted and mixture is smooth; cool.

2 Heat oven to 350°F. Grease or line cookie sheets with cooking parchment paper. In medium bowl, stir together flour, cocoa, baking soda and salt; set aside. In large bowl, beat 1 cup sugar, the eggs and vanilla with electric mixer on medium speed 2 minutes or until well blended. Add cooled chocolate mixture; beat on low speed until combined. Slowly beat in flour mixture until soft dough forms. Stir in toffee bits.

3 Shape dough into 1¼-inch balls. On ungreased cookie sheets, place balls about 2 inches apart. With bottom of glass dipped in sugar, flatten slightly.

4 Bake 8 to 10 minutes or until tops are dry (cookies will be soft in center). Cool 3 minutes; remove from cookie sheets to cooling racks. Cool completely before storing in tightly covered container.

1 Cookie: Calories 170; Total Fat 8g (Saturated Fat 4.5g, Trans Fat 0g); Cholesterol 25mg; Sodium 70mg; Total Carbohydrate 21g (Dietary Fiber 1g); Protein 2g **Exchanges:** ½ Starch, 1 Other Carbohydrate, 1½ Fat **Carbohydrate Choices:** 1½

Tip Flattening dough balls slightly before baking helps cookies bake more evenly.

Chocolate-Mint Layered Cookie Slices

Prep Time: 1 Hour 10 Minutes • **Start to Finish:** 4 Hours 40 Minutes • Makes 3½ dozen cookies

¾ cup butter or margarine, softened
¾ cup sugar
1 egg
1 teaspoon vanilla
2¼ cups Gold Medal all-purpose flour
¼ teaspoon baking powder
¼ teaspoon salt
1½ cups (9 oz) semisweet chocolate chips
1 tablespoon Gold Medal all-purpose flour
9 drops green food color
1 teaspoon mint extract
1 teaspoon shortening

1 In large bowl, beat butter and sugar with electric mixer on medium speed until creamy. Beat in egg and vanilla. On low speed, beat in 2¼ cups flour, the baking powder and salt until dough forms. Divide dough in half (about 1¼ cups each); place 1 portion in medium bowl.

2 In small microwavable bowl, microwave ½ cup of the chocolate chips on High 30 to 60 seconds or until melted, stirring twice. Stir until smooth; cool. Add melted chocolate to dough in medium bowl; knead until combined. To remaining dough, add 1 tablespoon flour, the food color and mint extract; mix until blended. Wrap each portion of dough in waxed paper; refrigerate 30 minutes.

3 Pat chocolate dough into rectangle shape. Place between sheets of cooking parchment paper. Roll to 10 x 6-inch rectangle, patting into shape with fingers as needed to retain rectangle shape. Repeat with green dough; remove top sheet of parchment paper. Remove top sheet of parchment paper from chocolate dough. Turn upside down over green dough, pressing firmly; remove parchment paper. With sharp knife or pizza cutter, cut lengthwise into 3 equal strips. Stack strips so you have 1 long rectangle, about 1½ inches high and 2 inches wide, pressing firmly. Wrap in plastic wrap; refrigerate 1 hour.

4 Heat oven to 350°F. Line cookie sheet with cooking parchment paper; set aside. Trim edges of dough log, if desired. Cut into ¼-inch slices. On lined cookie sheet, place slices about 2 inches apart. Bake 10 to 12 minutes or until edges start to brown. Remove from cookie sheets to cooling racks; cool completely.

5 In small microwavable bowl, microwave remaining 1 cup chocolate chips and the shortening uncovered on High 60 to 90 seconds or until melted, stirring twice. Stir until melted. Dip 1 edge of each cookie in chocolate. Place on cooking parchment paper; let stand until set, 1½ to 2 hours.

1 Cookie: Calories 100; Total Fat 5g (Saturated Fat 3g, Trans Fat 0g); Cholesterol 15mg; Sodium 45mg; Total Carbohydrate 13g (Dietary Fiber 0g); Protein 1g **Exchanges:** 1 Other Carbohydrate, 1 Fat **Carbohydrate Choices:** 1

Tip As with most refrigerator cookies, you can keep the dough in the refrigerator up to 1 week. Just bake part of the log, wrap up the rest and keep it for when you want fresh cookies. The dough can also be frozen up to 2 months.

Chocolate-Peppermint Shortbread

Prep Time: 15 Minutes • **Start to Finish:** 1 Hour 10 Minutes • Makes 32 cookies

Shortbread

1 cup butter or margarine, softened

½ cup granulated sugar

4 oz bittersweet baking chocolate, melted, cooled

½ teaspoon peppermint extract

2¼ cups Gold Medal all-purpose flour

⅓ cup unsweetened baking cocoa

Glaze and Topping

½ cup powdered sugar

2 tablespoons unsweetened baking cocoa

1 to 2 tablespoons milk

2 tablespoons chopped miniature peppermint candy canes

1 Heat oven to 325°F. Spray 2 (9-inch) glass pie plates with cooking spray.

2 In large bowl, beat butter, granulated sugar, chocolate and peppermint extract with electric mixer on medium speed until light and fluffy. On low speed, beat in flour and ⅓ cup cocoa. Divide dough in half. With lightly floured hands, press dough evenly in pie plates.

3 Bake 22 to 24 minutes or until edges just begin to pull away from sides of pie plates. Cool in pie plates 5 minutes. Carefully cut each round into 16 wedges. Cool completely in pie plates on cooling rack, about 30 minutes.

4 In small bowl, mix powdered sugar, 2 tablespoons cocoa and enough of the milk until glaze is smooth and thin enough to drizzle. Drizzle glaze over wedges; sprinkle with candies.

1 Cookie: Calories 140; Total Fat 8g (Saturated Fat 5g, Trans Fat 0g); Cholesterol 15mg; Sodium 45mg; Total Carbohydrate 15g (Dietary Fiber 1g); Protein 1g **Exchanges:** 1 Other Carbohydrate, 1½ Fat **Carbohydrate Choices:** 1

Tip Cut the rounds into wedges while they are warm, but do not remove them from the pie plates until they are completely cool so they won't break.

Shaped Cookies

Simple Turtle Cookie Cups

Prep Time: 45 Minutes • **Start to Finish:** 1 Hour 15 Minutes • Makes 3 dozen cookies

- 1 pouch (1 lb 1.5 oz) Betty Crocker double chocolate chunk cookie mix
- 3 tablespoons vegetable oil
- 1 tablespoon water
- 1 egg
- 36 round milk chocolate–covered chewy caramels, unwrapped
- 36 pecan halves

1 Heat oven to 375°F. Place miniature paper baking cup in each of 36 mini muffin cups.

2 In large bowl, stir cookie mix, oil, water and egg until soft dough forms. Shape dough into 1¼ inch balls; place 1 ball in each muffin cup.

3 Bake 8 to 9 minutes or until edges are set. Immediately press 1 milk chocolate–covered caramel into center of each cookie cup. Cool 2 minutes. Top each cookie cup with pecan half. Cool completely, about 30 minutes. Remove from pans with narrow spatula.

1 Cookie: Calories 110; Total Fat 5g (Saturated Fat 2g, Trans Fat 0g); Cholesterol 5mg; Sodium 75mg; Total Carbohydrate 15g (Dietary Fiber 0g); Protein 1g **Exchanges:** 1 Other Carbohydrate, 1 Fat **Carbohydrate Choices:** 1

Whoopie Pies

Prep Time: 45 Minutes • **Start to Finish:** 1 Hour 25 Minutes • Makes 1½ dozen whoopie pies

Cookies

1 cup granulated sugar
½ cup butter, softened
½ cup buttermilk
2 teaspoons vanilla
1 egg
2 oz unsweetened baking chocolate, melted, cooled
1¾ cups Gold Medal all-purpose flour
½ teaspoon baking soda
½ teaspoon salt

Filling

3 cups powdered sugar
1 jar (7 oz) marshmallow creme
¾ cup butter, softened
6 to 7 teaspoons milk

1 Heat oven to 400°F. Grease cookie sheets with shortening or cooking spray, or line with cooking parchment paper.

2 In large bowl, beat granulated sugar, ½ cup butter, the buttermilk, vanilla, egg and chocolate with electric mixer on medium speed, or mix with spoon. Stir in flour, baking soda and salt. Onto cookie sheets, drop dough by rounded tablespoonfuls about 2 inches apart.

3 Bake 8 to 10 minutes or until almost no indentation remains when touched in center. Immediately remove from cookie sheets to cooling racks. Cool completely, about 30 minutes.

4 In large bowl, beat all filling ingredients on medium speed about 2 minutes or until light and fluffy. For each whoopie pie, spread slightly less than 3 tablespoons filling, on bottom of 1 cooled cookie. Top with second cookie, bottom side down; gently press cookies together. Store in tightly covered container.

1 Whoopie Pie: Calories 350; Total Fat 15g (Saturated Fat 9g, Trans Fat 0.5g); Cholesterol 45mg; Sodium 210mg; Total Carbohydrate 50g (Dietary Fiber 1g); Protein 2g **Exchanges:** 1 Starch, 2½ Other Carbohydrate, 3 Fat **Carbohydrate Choices:** 3

Chocolate Chip Whoopie Pies: Fold ½ cup miniature semisweet chocolate chips intothe filling.

Pink Peppermint Whoopie Pies:
Add 6 drops red food color to filling ingredients.Once cookies are assembled, sprinkle edges of filling with crushed peppermint candies or candy canes.

Toffee Whoopie Pies: Fold ½ cup milk chocolate–covered toffee bits into the filling.

Chocolate-Mallow Cookie Pies

Prep Time: 50 Minutes • **Start to Finish:** 1 Hour 10 Minutes • Makes 1½ dozen sandwich cookies

1 Heat oven to 350°F. In large bowl, stir together cookie mix, cocoa and flour. Add sour cream, ¼ cup butter, 1 teaspoon vanilla and the egg; stir until stiff dough forms.

2 Shape dough into 1-inch balls. On ungreased cookie sheets, place balls about 2 inches apart. Press each ball to flatten slightly.

3 Bake 8 to 9 minutes or until set (do not overbake). Cool 2 minutes; remove from cookie sheets to cooling racks. Cool completely, about 15 minutes.

4 In small bowl, beat all filling ingredients with electric mixer until light and fluffy. For each cookie pie, spread about 2 teaspoons filling on bottom of 1 cooled cookie. Top with second cookie, bottom side down; gently press cookies together.

5 In small bowl, stir together all topping ingredients; sprinkle over tops of cookie pies. Store between sheets of waxed paper in tightly covered container.

Cookies
- 1 pouch (1 lb 1.5 oz) Betty Crocker sugar cookie mix
- ⅓ cup unsweetened baking cocoa
- 2 tablespoons Gold Medal all-purpose flour
- ⅓ cup sour cream
- ¼ cup butter or margarine, softened
- 1 teaspoon vanilla
- 1 egg

Filling
- ⅔ cup marshmallow creme
- ⅓ cup butter, softened
- ½ teaspoon vanilla
- ⅔ cup powdered sugar

Topping
- 1 tablespoon powdered sugar
- ⅛ teaspoon unsweetened baking cocoa

1 Sandwich Cookie: Calories 220; Total Fat 10g (Saturated Fat 5g, Trans Fat 1.5g); Cholesterol 30mg; Sodium 130mg; Total Carbohydrate 31g (Dietary Fiber 0g); Protein 2g **Exchanges:** 1 Starch, 1 Other Carbohydrate, 2 Fat **Carbohydrate Choices:** 2

Tip To easily scoop marshmallow creme out of the jar, lightly spray a rubber spatula with cooking spray.

Metric Conversion Guide

Volume

U.S. Units	Canadian Metric	Australian Metric
¼ teaspoon	1 mL	1 ml
½ teaspoon	2 mL	2 ml
1 teaspoon	5 mL	5 ml
1 tablespoon	15 mL	20 ml
¼ cup	50 mL	60 ml
⅓ cup	75 mL	80 ml
½ cup	125 mL	125 ml
⅔ cup	150 mL	170 ml
¾ cup	175 mL	190 ml
1 cup	250 mL	250 ml
1 quart	1 liter	1 liter
1½ quarts	1.5 liters	1.5 liters
2 quarts	2 liters	2 liters
2½ quarts	2.5 liters	2.5 liters
3 quarts	3 liters	3 liters
4 quarts	4 liters	4 liters

Weight

U.S. Units	Canadian Metric	Australian Metric
1 ounce	30 grams	30 grams
2 ounces	55 grams	60 grams
3 ounces	85 grams	90 grams
4 ounces (¼ pound)	115 grams	125 grams
8 ounces (½ pound)	225 grams	225 grams
16 ounces (1 pound)	455 grams	500 grams
1 pound	455 grams	0.5 kilogram

Note: The recipes in this cookbook have not been developed or tested using metric measures. When converting recipes to metric, some variations in quality may be noted.

Measurements

Inches	Centimeters
1	2.5
2	5.0
3	7.5
4	10.0
5	12.5
6	15.0
7	17.5
8	20.5
9	23.0
10	25.5
11	28.0
12	30.5
13	33.0

Temperatures

Fahrenheit	Celsius
32°	0°
212°	100°
250°	120°
275°	140°
300°	150°
325°	160°
350°	180°
375°	190°
400°	200°
425°	220°
450°	230°
475°	240°
500°	260°

Recipe Testing and Calculating Nutrition Information

Recipe Testing:

- Large eggs and 2% milk were used unless otherwise indicated.
- Fat-free, low-fat, low-sodium or lite products were not used unless indicated.
- No nonstick cookware and bakeware were used unless otherwise indicated. No dark-colored, black or insulated bakeware was used.
- When a pan is specified, a metal pan was used; a baking dish or pie plate means ovenproof glass was used.
- An electric hand mixer was used for mixing only when mixer speeds are specified.

Calculating Nutrition:

- The first ingredient was used wherever a choice is given, such as ⅓ cup sour cream or plain yogurt.
- The first amount was used wherever a range is given, such as 3- to 3½-pound whole chicken.
- The first serving number was used wherever a range is given, such as 4 to 6 servings.
- "If desired" ingredients were not included.
- Only the amount of a marinade or frying oil that is absorbed was included.

America's most trusted cookbook is better than ever!

- 1,100 all-new photos, including hundreds of step-by-step images
- More than 1,500 recipes, with hundreds of inspiring variations and creative "mini" recipes for easy cooking ideas
- Brand-new features
- Gorgeous new design

Get the best edition of the *Betty Crocker Cookbook* today!

www.ingramcontent.com/pod-product-compliance
Lightning Source LLC
Chambersburg PA
CBHW071417290426
44108CB00014B/1869